Who Is
Megan Rapinoe?

Who Is
Megan Rapinoe?

by Stefanie Loh

illustrated by Andrew Thomson

Penguin Workshop

To Samantha Fern—may you, like Megan,
always have the courage to be yourself and stand up
for what you believe in. To my wife, Lauren, Mom,
Tiff, Nancy, Amanda, Kim, Joe, Katie, Sarah,
Mel, and Andrea: Thank you for gifting me
the time to write this—SL

For Rhia and Cerys—AT

PENGUIN WORKSHOP
An imprint of Penguin Random House LLC, New York

First published in the United States of America by Penguin Workshop,
an imprint of Penguin Random House LLC, New York, 2023

Visit us online at penguinrandomhouse.com.

Library of Congress Control Number: 2022042067

Printed in the United States of America

ISBN 9780593520802 (paperback)   10 9 8 7 6 5 4 3 2 1 WOR
ISBN 9780593520819 (library binding)   10 9 8 7 6 5 4 3 2 1 WOR

Contents

Who Is Megan Rapinoe?

The pressure was on as the United States Women's National Team (USWNT) took the field on June 28, 2019, for the FIFA Women's World Cup quarterfinal against France. The US team entered the tournament ranked number one in the world, after going undefeated in seventeen matches in the year leading up to this World Cup. But France had broken the Americans' unbeaten streak with a 3–1 win in a friendly match in January. Now, they'd play again with a semifinal spot at stake.

With her pink hair, easy smile, and wicked goal-scoring abilities, American striker Megan Rapinoe had become one of the fan favorites of the USWNT as the Americans blazed through the tournament. Megan had scored two exciting goals to power her team through their round of sixteen matches against Spain. And now, she was determined to help bring them into the semifinals.

The Parc des Princes stadium in Paris was packed to capacity with more than forty-five thousand people as Megan put the Americans ahead in the fifth minute with a free-kick goal from twenty-two yards out. The ball snuck through the legs of the players jostling in front of the goal and slotted neatly into the corner. Even though France was the host nation, American fans filled the stands, and as they roared to celebrate the goal, Megan proudly spun toward the fans and threw open her arms with a wide grin on her face in a now-famous pose.

But Megan wasn't done. She struck again when Tobin Heath sent the ball rocketing to an onrushing Megan, who scored from eight yards out! That put the US up 2–0. And even though the French would score on a free kick in the eighty-first minute, they never caught up. At the final whistle, Megan and her teammates celebrated wildly. Megan's goals had sent them to the semifinals!

The triumphant pose Megan struck after her first goal against France became known as her power pose, and it appeared everywhere in photos and news articles about the Americans' big semifinal win over the host nation. It was printed on posters, mugs, and T-shirts. As the US Women's National Team rolled to a gold medal in the World Cup, this bold lesbian striker with a big personality and an air of fearlessness both on and off the pitch would transcend her sport to become known as an activist and a legend.

CHAPTER 1
Young Megan

Megan Rapinoe and her twin sister, Rachael (fraternal twins do not look alike), were born on July 5, 1985, in Redding, California. The twins were the youngest of six children, and they were inseparable. They spent their childhood running around the empty field across from the house, riding bikes, playing hide-and-seek and laser tag, and catching crawdads at the nearby creek.

The girls particularly looked up to their older brother Brian, who played soccer. They wandered the sidelines at Brian's practices, watching and copying his moves. At age six, they joined a boys' Under-8 soccer team because there were no girls' teams close by. The twins didn't mind. They loved soccer, and they happened to be naturally good at it. Megan and Rachael dominated the boys on their team, playing so well that their coach declared to their parents, Denise and Jim, "They're going to be in the World Cup one day!"

The Rapinoe twins' secret? Even though they were best friends, they were also each other's biggest rivals, and they got better by challenging each other. Every day after school until sunset, the twins practiced their soccer skills in the yard or at a nearby soccer field.

But off the soccer field, the girls were very different. Megan was a goofball with a knack for doing funny impressions of people, while Rachael was quiet and more serious. By sixth grade, Rachael was very social and had lots of friends, while Megan considered herself a tomboy who didn't quite fit in. She counted on Rachael to help her.

The twins played on boys' soccer teams until they were ten. Then their father started a girls' team that he coached for a few years. After that, the twins were invited to join the competitive Elk Grove club soccer team, based in Sacramento, about a two-hour drive south of their home. So every weekend morning until the twins were about seventeen, Denise and Jim packed the girls into the family minivan at 4 a.m. to take them to Sacramento for practices or games. The twins embraced this busy life because by this time they were both soccer fanatics. And the 1999 FIFA Women's World Cup only fed that fire.

The 1999 Women's World Cup was the third edition of the tournament and the first to be played in the United States. Megan and Rachael watched the games on television, thrilled to see their favorite sport being played in front of thousands of cheering people. The sisters even got to see the US beat Brazil in person when they attended the semifinal game at Stanford Stadium. Amid an exciting atmosphere, the US won 2–0 and advanced to the final.

Watching the team's journey to its second World Cup title after beating China in the finals made a huge impression on Megan. She and Rachael were just two of the thousands of girls who idolized the USWNT stars after the World Cup. That summer, Megan and Rachael put up a poster of the Women's National Team on their bedroom wall. They dreamed of playing college soccer, but Megan never imagined that she might one day be featured in a similar poster wearing the red, white, and blue jersey of the US national team.

CHAPTER 2
College and Early Days with the National Team

By their senior year of high school, Rachael and Megan were being recruited by many colleges to play soccer. None of the schools really felt "right" until they visited the University of Portland, in Oregon, in fall 2003. The Portland Pilots, had won a national championship in 2002. Also, the twins liked the school and the city, and they felt like they fit in with the team. They accepted full scholarship offers to the University of Portland and planned to start their freshman year of college there in September 2004.

Then, Megan got a phone call. The coach of the US Women's National Team wanted her to represent the US in the FIFA Under-19 Women's

World Championship in Thailand. (FIFA is the governing organization for soccer worldwide.) Megan was stunned that the national team was even aware of her!

So in fall 2004, the twins separated for the first time, each happy for the other but excited to begin her own journey. Rachael started college in Portland, while Megan deferred (put off) college for a term to play with the U-19 national team.

Megan scored three goals in the U-19 Women's World Championship series. Over three weeks in Thailand, she played in front of international fans and befriended players such as Ashlyn Harris and Becky Sauerbrunn, who became lifelong friends. Megan had gotten her first taste of life as a professional soccer player (someone who is paid to play soccer), and she wanted more. Could she make the national team in time for the 2007 FIFA Women's World Cup or the 2008 Olympics?

Becky Sauerbrunn   Megan Rapinoe

But first, Megan joined Rachael in college, enrolling at Portland in January 2005 and instantly becoming one of the Pilots' stars. Portland went undefeated during the 2005 season and won its second national championship in four years. Megan started every game that season and scored fifteen goals. She finished her first season of college soccer as an All-American and was named the Soccer Times National Freshman of the Year.

Living away from home for the first time also helped Megan get to know herself in a different way. A few weeks into freshman year, Megan developed a crush on one of her teammates. As she explored her emotions, she realized she was gay. "For the first time, I was attracted to someone, and the discovery thrilled me," Megan wrote in her autobiography. She rushed out to share the news with Rachael. And her response was simply: "Oh, me too." Once again, the twins realized they were so in tune that they couldn't surprise each other!

College wasn't all rosy for Megan, however. Expectations were high after her successful freshman year—especially after she finished training camp with the US senior national team. At camp, she shared a locker room with national team greats like Kate Markgraf, and also Kristine Lilly, whom she remembered cheering on during the 1999 Women's World Cup. Megan couldn't believe she was now on their team! She did well in camp and played in two international friendly matches afterward. But in a game for Portland that fall, Megan injured her left knee. The diagnosis was a torn anterior cruciate ligament (ACL), and the doctor told Megan she would need surgery and that her sophomore season was over.

After surgery, Megan worked hard in physical therapy to strengthen her knee and pushed herself relentlessly, trying to beat the doctor's estimates and get back on the field faster. She was cleared to play again to start her junior year, only to repeat the same injury in practice a few weeks into the season. For the second time in a year, Megan had surgery on her left knee. When she woke up in bed after this second surgery, her mom said gently, "You know, Megan, it's not the end of the world. You still have your college scholarship, and you've achieved great things already." But Megan refused to believe that knee problems might have ended her promising soccer career. "Mom, I'm not done," she said.

Her determination paid off. Megan forced herself to be more patient with her recovery. She followed her doctor's orders. And she trained for about a year and a half without playing in any games. Megan returned to competition in the Pilots' 2008 season opener against Oregon that August, notching two assists. It was the start of a great season for Portland, which won nineteen straight games before losing in the semifinals of the national tournament.

After graduating from college, Megan was drafted by the Chicago Red Stars, a team in the new Women's Professional Soccer (WPS) league, in which teams in different American cities play one another. She moved to Chicago that March, thrilled that playing soccer was now her job!

CHAPTER 3
Becoming an Activist

Megan loved her new life as a professional soccer player. Aside from starting nineteen games with the Red Stars, she was also playing some international games with the US Women's National Team. She'd done it! Her recovery and comeback from two knee injuries was complete!

Megan also started dating a fellow pro soccer player named Sarah Walsh, who was from Australia but played for another WPS team. Megan and Sarah never hid their relationship. As Megan puts it, "I was out to everyone on the team, and I was out to my family, and beyond that, no one was asking."

Megan and Sarah were dating when a push to make marriage accessible to gay people had begun in the United States. In 2010, even though a few states had legalized gay marriage, the US federal government still only recognized marriage as between a man and a woman. Because of that, if, for example, an Australian citizen like Sarah had married an American citizen like Megan, Sarah would not have been able to get US citizenship because she was a woman. But as the fight to allow LGBTQ+ people to marry and be acknowledged by the federal government gained steam, the issue began to feel increasingly personal to Megan.

Megan was excited to make the US team for the 2011 FIFA Women's World Cup and was determined to prove herself. Megan's first opportunity came in the United States' second World Cup game, against Colombia. She came off the bench and scored almost immediately! Then, in the United States' quarterfinal game against Brazil, she made a huge play. With the US team trailing Brazil 2–1 in the game's dying moments, Megan corralled a pass from Carli Lloyd and shot it up the field to Abby Wambach, who headed the ball into the goal for the tying score! The game

Abby Wambach

went to a penalty shoot-out, and the US won 5–3 after Megan, Abby, Carli, and two other players made successful penalty-kick goals! Megan and Abby were both hailed as heroes!

The 2011 Women's World Cup saw a huge increase in audience numbers. In the US, 14 million people watched on TV when the women played Japan in the final—a very close game that went to a penalty shoot-out. Japan won, sending the US women home in disappointment. But something amazing had happened: people were paying attention to women's soccer in numbers never seen before.

On the plane back home, Megan thought about all these things. How LGBTQ+ (lesbian, gay, bisexual, transgender, and queer or questioning) people in the US were still fighting for the right to marry the person they loved. How she'd made a name for herself in this World Cup, and how, despite losing to Japan in the final, her team had generated so much attention that they were returning home with the spotlight on them. If she was going to be famous and able to influence people, she wanted to be celebrated for *all* of who she was. Megan decided that before the 2012 London Olympics, she would come out (which means to declare something publicly) as a lesbian because keeping her sexuality hidden just didn't feel right anymore. She thought it was important that gay people everywhere could see other gay people represented in public life.

Megan came out the following July, right before the 2012 Olympics, in an interview with *Out Magazine*. "People want—they *need*—to see that there are people like me playing soccer for the good ol' U.S. of A.," Megan said in the article. From that point, Megan used her celebrity as a professional soccer player to advocate for gay rights.

The women had hoped that their popularity after the World Cup would help grow the popularity of the Women's Professional Soccer league. But by the time Megan and her USWNT teammates flew to London for the 2012 Olympics,

the league had shut down. And the women had started to question the fairness of the US Soccer Federation.

The US Women's National Team was ranked No. 1 in the world entering the Olympics. The men's team was ranked thirty-sixth, and they had not even qualified for the Olympics. So, why did the women make less money than the men? The US Soccer Federation's pay system was obviously unfair. But for the USWNT to make the public care about the issue, they knew they had to keep winning.

CHAPTER 4
Raising the Profile of Women's Soccer

That motivation propelled the US women to the 2012 Olympic finals, where they played Japan again. This time, the United States was

victorious, with Carli Lloyd scoring two goals to clinch a 2–1 win and an Olympic gold medal!

The team was greeted as champions when they returned to the United States. Their win raised the profile of women's soccer, and a new professional league was born: the National Women's Soccer League (NWSL). Coming off their Olympic gold medals, the US national team players were

celebrities, and there was an air of optimism around the new NWSL. Everyone hoped this league would succeed even though the one before it had failed. This time, Megan was signed by the Seattle Reign. From the beginning, she was one of the Reign's biggest stars. She helped the new league gain popularity and also made Seattle her home.

Megan and the US women were now training for the 2015 Women's World Cup, which would be played in Canada. The women's recent successes had earned them millions of fans, and they used that popularity in their continued fight to be treated as equals with the men's soccer team. The US women were still being paid less than the players on the US men's team. For example, the women received $50 for expenses per travel day, while the men got $62.50. If the men lost a friendly match, they still earned $5,000 each. Each woman on the national team made only

$1,350 for a *win*. This was particularly frustrating for Megan and her teammates because they had outperformed the US men: They had won two World Cups and four Olympic gold medals. The men had never finished higher than third in the World Cup (and that was in 1930!), and they had never won Olympic gold.

Even the international soccer community treated women's teams as inferior to men's teams. The men's World Cup was always played on real grass, a much gentler surface, while the women's games at the 2015 World Cup were to be played on rough artificial turf. The women felt insulted. A group of women from various international teams filed a complaint, but nothing changed. Once again, the US women felt that for them to make real change, they had to keep winning.

Megan and her teammates fought their way to the World Cup final against Japan. In the second minute, Megan lofted a corner kick to Carli

Lloyd, who scored what would be the first of her three goals against Japan. When the final whistle blew, the US team had crushed Japan 5–2!

The team returned home victorious and used their fame to push for change. In all media interviews, they talked about the lack of equal pay for women. With Megan, Carli, Hope Solo, Alex Morgan, and Becky Sauerbrunn leading the way, they filed a lawsuit against the US Soccer Federation. Now a national team veteran, Megan embraced her role as a leader and activist.

CHAPTER 5
Taking a Knee

In December 2015, Megan once again needed surgery, but this time on her right knee.

Luckily, Megan recovered from the injury in time to make the 2016 Olympic team. But in the quarterfinals, the experienced Swedish team proved too much for the Americans, who lost 4–3. It was the earliest elimination from the Olympics the US women had ever suffered.

But something wonderful came out of that summer in Brazil. After Megan's team lost, she stayed to watch the rest of the Olympics as a spectator. One night, at a party with the gold medal–winning US women's basketball team, Megan met Sue Bird, the team's star point guard, who also played for the Seattle Storm of the

Women's National Basketball Association. Megan and Sue hit it off instantly. Their friendship blossomed at a time when Megan would find herself most in need of support, because the rest of 2016 brought many challenges.

As Megan became more involved in the fight for LGBTQ+ rights, her interest in how other people have been treated unfairly grew. When an unarmed Black American teenager named Michael Brown was killed by a white police officer while walking down a street in Missouri in 2014, Megan became horrified by how unjustly Black Americans are treated because of their skin color. In the summer of 2016, protests broke out across the US and public anger about the mistreatment of Black people by police spread to the sports world. One of the most notable examples was NFL quarterback Colin Kaepernick, who started kneeling instead of standing during the pregame national anthem. Kaepernick, who is Black, said he did not want to stand to honor the flag of a country that treats Black people and people of color unfairly.

Megan was moved by Kaepernick's gesture. She loved her country, and she felt it was important to protest racism. So that September, after Kaepernick started kneeling during the national anthem, Megan did the same. She took a knee before Seattle Reign games, and also before the US national team's games. Megan's kneeling during the anthem made many people mad. Some felt that she was disrespecting the US flag or the US military. Others wrote mean things to her on social media. But Megan kept it up. To her, kneeling during the anthem was a visible way to protest the mistreatment of Black people in America.

It helped that Megan had a good friend supporting her. Since the Olympics, Megan and Sue Bird had grown closer, and Sue understood

Megan in a way that no one else ever had.
Sue was steady and measured, while Megan was
more likely to react quickly. So even after the US
women's national team coach benched Megan
because she would not agree to stand during the

anthem, Sue's advice helped Megan keep her cool and not say anything to her coach that she might regret. But Megan was kept off the national team for months—largely, she suspected, because of her kneeling during the anthem.

In many ways, Sue and Megan were opposites. Megan had always relied on her natural talent to stand out on the soccer pitch. While equally talented, Sue followed a strict training routine and diet. The more Megan hung out with Sue, the more she followed Sue's example and ate healthier and trained harder. In turn, Megan made Sue, a very private person, more comfortable with her own sexuality and more willing to talk about it publicly. The two women were quickly falling in love.

CHAPTER 6
New Beginnings

By spring 2017, Megan had not played for the national team in more than six months, even though she was fully recovered from her knee injury. Privately, Megan wondered if her international soccer career might be over. As she began her professional season with the Seattle Reign, Megan decided that the best way to play herself back onto the national team was to dazzle the National Women's Soccer League. She wanted the national coaches to notice her. Megan scored twelve goals in seventeen starts for the Reign, and the national team could not keep the NWSL's hottest star off the US roster. That July, Megan earned her first national team start since September 2016.

With Megan back, the team began a hot streak. From January through November 2018, the American women went undefeated, with Megan's goal and assist tally rising to a career-high nineteen. Her training with Sue and her patience had paid off. Now, Megan wanted to make a statement. Even Sue was shocked when Megan decided to dye her blond hair pink the day before she left for the 2019 World Cup in France!

Going into the World Cup, the spotlight was on the US women's fight for equal pay. Once again, the players knew that winning on a big stage would help them gain public support in their legal case against the US Soccer Federation. The American team found themselves up against a surprising critic—the president of the United States, Donald Trump, who had opposed many issues Megan thought were important. When reporters asked Megan, the team's cocaptain, whether the national team would follow the tradition of championship teams visiting the White House if they won the World Cup, she said no. This angered the president, who declared that Megan had disrespected her country.

Pink hair blazing, Megan scored two huge goals against France in the quarterfinals. In the final, she struck again—knocking in a penalty-kick goal to help the US beat the Netherlands 2–0 and win their fourth World Cup title! Megan finished the World Cup with six goals and was awarded the Golden Boot, which goes to the tournament's top goal scorer, and the Golden Ball, which goes to the tournament's best player. The US women returned home to a heroes' welcome and a victory parade in New York City. (True to their word, the team declined an invitation to visit the White House.)

The 2019 World Cup made Megan a superstar. Her pink hair and her power pose inspired young

soccer players everywhere. And in fall 2020, while they were on vacation, she proposed to Sue.

After Megan and the US women won a bronze medal at the 2020 Tokyo Olympics, reporters asked Megan if she was retiring from international competition. "I don't really know yet," she said. "I need to take some time to think about it." But even if Megan never competes in another World Cup, she's already made her name as one of the best to ever play the game. She's scored sixty-two international goals in 187 appearances with the US women's team. She's won two World Cup gold medals, one Olympic gold and one Olympic bronze, and in 2019 was named the year's Best FIFA Women's Player and awarded the Ballon d'Or, which goes to the world's best women's soccer player.

But the impact she's made off the field is just as much a part of Megan's legacy. In 2020, Megan was named one of *TIME* magazine's 100 Most

Influential People. The equal pay lawsuit she helped to lead against the US Soccer Federation was settled in February 2022. The federation agreed to pay the players $22 million, with an extra $2 million being set aside to help players after their careers are over. More importantly, the federation has agreed to pay the men's and women's teams equally going forward. Megan has worked hard for equal pay, gay rights, and Black rights. In July 2022, President Joe Biden awarded Megan the Presidential Medal of Freedom, all but ensuring that her legacy will last far beyond her time on the field.

History of the US Women's National Team

The United States women's national soccer team is widely regarded as the world's most successful women's soccer team.

The program started in 1985, when the US Soccer Federation asked Mike Ryan to assemble a women's team for a tournament in Italy. That team finished the tournament in fourth place. In 1991, the US won the first FIFA Women's World Cup by beating Norway 2–1. The USWNT also won the first women's soccer Olympic gold medal when the sport was added to the Olympics lineup at the 1996 Olympics in Atlanta, Georgia.

In 1999, the US hosted the Women's World Cup, and that gold medal–winning USWNT, including players Mia Hamm and Brandi Chastain, inspired an entire generation of American girls to play soccer, accelerating the sport's growth in the United States.

The US has remained a women's soccer powerhouse. The Americans have won four FIFA Women's World Cups. The USWNT also won Olympic gold in 2004, 2008, and 2012, and has been ranked No. 1 in the FIFA Women's World Rankings for fourteen out of the twenty years of the rankings' existence.

Timeline of Megan Rapinoe's Life

1985 — Megan Rapinoe and her fraternal twin, Rachael, are born on July 5, in Redding, California

2002 — At age sixteen, Megan is selected to play a game in France with the US Under-17 Women's National Team

2004 — Along with Rachael, accepts scholarship offer to play soccer at the University of Portland

— Plays in the FIFA U-19 Women's World Championship series

2011 — Plays in all six FIFA World Cup games

2012 — Comes out as a lesbian in an interview with *Out Magazine*

— Wins gold at the 2012 London Olympics

2015 — Wins gold at FIFA World Cup, beating Japan in final

2016 — Plays in the 2016 Olympics in Rio de Janeiro

— Decides to take a knee during the pregame national anthem

2019 — Plays with the USWNT to win gold in the FIFA World Cup and wins the Golden Boot and Golden Ball

— Named *Sports Illustrated*'s Sportsperson of the Year

2020 — Named one of *TIME* magazine's 100 Most Influential People

— Gets engaged to Sue Bird

2021 — Plays with the USWNT at the 2020 Tokyo Olympics

2022 — Awarded the Presidential Medal of Freedom

Timeline of the World

1989 — The Berlin Wall, which divided East and West Berlin, is torn down

1994 — Amazon.com is founded by Jeff Bezos out of his garage in Bellevue, Washington, starting out as an online bookseller

1998 — The first module of the International Space Station is launched from Baikonur Cosmodrome, Kazakhstan

2001 — Two planes are flown into the World Trade Center in New York City by terrorists on September 11, with a third plane striking the Pentagon in Washington, DC, and a fourth plane diverted, crashing in a field in at Shanksville, Pennsylvania

2004 — Massachusetts becomes the first state in the US to legalize same-sex marriage

2015 — One hundred and ninety-five countries commit to lowering greenhouse gas emissions to stave off climate change in a deal that will become known as the Paris Agreement

2020 — NASA launches the *Perseverance* rover, sending it to Mars for research purposes

2021 — A mob storms the US Capitol in a failed attempt to demand that lawmakers not ratify the results of the 2020 presidential election

Bibliography

*Books for young readers

Carmichael, Emma. "Megan Rapinoe and Sue Bird Are Goals." *GQ Magazine*. February 9, 2021. https://www.gq.com/story/megan-rapinoe-sue-bird-march-modern-lovers-cover.

Chappell, Bill. "U.S. Women's Soccer Team Members File Federal Equal-Pay Complaint." *NPR*. March 31, 2016. https://www.npr.org/sections/thetwo-way/2016/03/31/472522790/members-of-u-s-women-s-national-team-file-federal-equal-pay-complaint.

Goff, Steven, and Emily Giambalvo. "U.S. Wins World Cup with a Final Four-Star Performance." *The Washington Post*. July 7, 2019. https://www.washingtonpost.com/sports/2019/07/07/uswnt-netherlands-world-cup-final/.

Linehan, Meg. *Secrets of Success: Insights from Megan Rapinoe's World-Class Soccer Career*. New York: Skyhorse Publishing, 2021.

Portwood, Jerry. "Fever Pitch: As an Out U.S. Olympic Soccer Player, Megan Rapinoe's Got Balls." *Out Magazine*. July 2, 2012. https://www.out.com/travel-nightlife/london/2012/07/02/fever-pitch.

Rapinoe, Megan. *One Life*. New York: Penguin Books, 2021.

*Rapinoe, Megan. *One Life: Megan Rapinoe, International Soccer Star and Activist—Young Readers Edition*. New York: Penguin Random House, 2021.

Rapinoe, Megan. "You Can't Get Rid of Your Girl That Easily." *The Players' Tribune*. June 23, 2019. https://www. theplayerstribune.com/articles/megan-rapinoe-united-states-world-cup-youre-not-gonna-get-rid-of-your-girl-that-easily.

US Soccer Communications Department. *U.S. Women's National Team 2022 Media Guide*. Chicago: ABC Printing, 2022.

Vrentas, Jenny. "2019 Sportsperson of the Year: Megan Rapinoe." *Sports Illustrated*. December 9, 2019. https://www. si.com/sportsperson/2019/12/09/megan-rapinoe-2019-sportsperson-of-the-year.

YOUR HEADQUARTERS FOR HISTORY

Activities, Mad Libs, and sidesplitting jokes!
Discover the Who HQ books beyond the biographies

Who? What? Where?

Learn more at whohq.com!